This Book Belongs to:

_____

Ask the Archbishop

By Archbishop Bernard Hebda

and the Catholic grade school children from the
Archdiocese of Saint Paul and Minneapolis

CATHOLIC SCHOOLS
CEN†ER OF EXCELLENCE

© Catholic Schools Center of Excellence
3033 Excelsior Boulevard, Suite 550
Minneapolis, MN 55416
https://cscoe-mn.org
https://findcatholicschools.org

Editor: Melissa Hamilton
Designer: Danielle Rother
Publishing and Production Management: Jim Bindas, Books & Projects LLC
Proofreaders: Terri Lee Paulsen and Louise Kertesz

Distributed by the Catholic Schools Center of Excellence
3033 Excelsior Boulevard, Suite 550
Minneapolis, MN 55416

ISBN: 978-1-5323-6312-2

Cover Image: Maisie Rix, Presentation of the Blessed Virgin Mary, Maplewood, MN
Inside Back Cover Photo: Bob Cunningham
Back Cover Photo: Andy King

Printed in China

"Jesus said, 'Let the little children come to me' for a good reason. Their innocence, openness and perspective on life can be a real source of blessing and insight for the Church."
– Archbishop Bernard Hebda

This book of letters is meant to shine a light on the faith journey of children with Christ as they reveal their questions, thoughts and hopes with us. We took our idea to Archbishop Hebda, and we were thrilled when he agreed to partner with us on this journey. We moved ahead and created lesson plans to support the dedicated teachers in the Archdiocese of Saint Paul and Minneapolis to take the next step in helping their students craft letters to share what was on their minds and in their hearts.

Through the hundreds of letters we received from students, we were reminded and renewed in our belief that our future leaders' faith is being nourished each and every day. It was very difficult to choose from the many beautiful responses we received, but we could not be prouder of what we have here — a voice from each school that participated.

Thank you to everyone who supported us on this joyful journey.

– Michelle Schlehuber, Jeanne Doyle and Steve Wright
Convent of the Visitation School in Mendota Heights, MN

Luke

Nativity of Our Lord
Catholic School
Saint Paul, MN

First Grade

"Does God really love us when we make mistakes?"

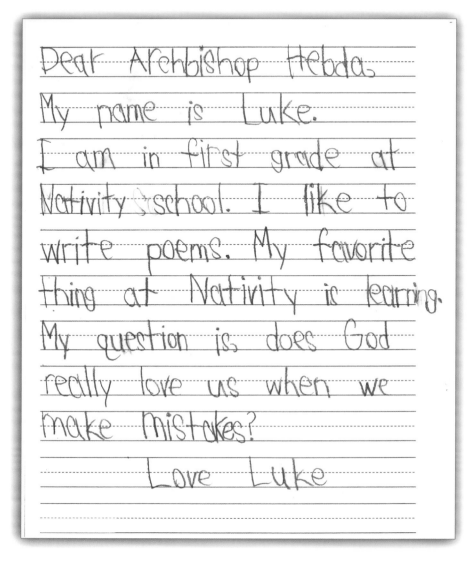

Dear Archbishop Hebda,
My name is Luke.
I am in first grade at Nativity school. I like to write poems. My favorite thing at Nativity is learning. My question is, does God really love us when we make mistakes?

Love Luke

ARCHDIOCESE
OF
SAINT PAUL &
MINNEAPOLIS

Dear Luke,

The more that we learn about the life of Jesus, the easier it is to believe that we have a God who loves us always, even when we make mistakes. In fact, it seems that Jesus had a special love for those who made mistakes. St. Peter, for example, made lots of mistakes and yet the Lord made him the head of the Church. As a group, the Apostles often seemed like real bumblers, and yet the Lord loved them deeply.

The Cross is where we see God's love for us most clearly. Imagine that Jesus would be willing to give his last breath for those of us who sin and make lots of mistakes. One of the last things that Jesus said was, "Father, forgive them, they know not what they do." That gives me, a sinner who makes mistakes, great hope.

+Bernard A. Hebda

Harriet

Carondelet Catholic School
Minneapolis, MN

Fourth Grade

"Do you know what our guardian angels look like? Are they possibly human? Also, can people who have died look down at you from heaven?"

Dear Archbishop Hebda,
        My name is Harriet and I am in 4th grade at Carondelet Catholic School. I like to swim and do gymnastics. A few of my hobbies are knitting, sewing, and reading.
        I have a few questions for you. Do you know what our guardian angels look like? Are they possibly human? Also can people who have died look down at you from heaven? I have been wondering these for a while and I hope that you can answer them!
        Thank you so much for reading this letter! You are an amazing person and have done so much in your life. Thank you so much for all you have done!

Sincerely, Harriet

ARCHDIOCESE
OF
SAINT PAUL &
MINNEAPOLIS

Dear Harriet,

I have never seen my guardian angel. But I know that he has to be strong because he has managed to get me out of some very difficult situations.

In paintings, artists often make angels look like human beings — but while angels and people are both created by God, they are very different. On the positive side, an angel is never going to have a sore knee or suffer from a spider bite. On the negative side, I have a feeling that God loves us way more than He loves the angels, because He sent his son Jesus to take on our flesh and to save us, even at the cost of his life. That's real love.

As for whether people who have died can look down from heaven, I think the answer has to be a "yes." I often feel the presence of my parents, for example, just at the right time. They seem to know from heaven just when I need their encouragement. Our Church has always taught, moreover, that we can turn to the saints in heaven to help us along the way. They too see and hear us in our need.

+Bernard A. Hebda

Raphael

Blessed Trinity Catholic School
Richfield, MN

Fifth Grade

"When did you get a feeling that God wanted you to become a priest? I've got a problem with an older brother. How would you handle this problem?"

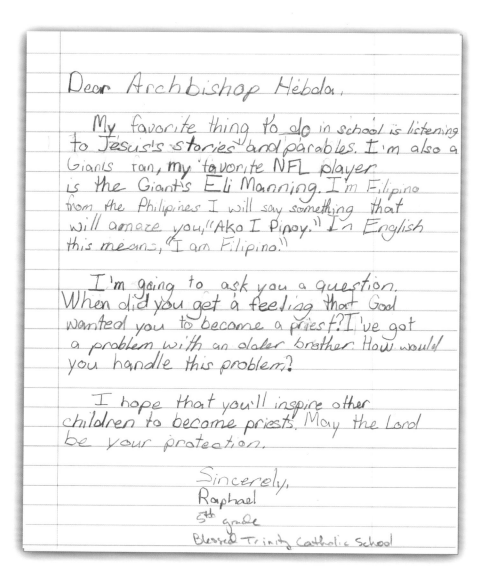

Dear Archbishop Hebda,

My favorite thing to do in school is listening to Jesus's stories and parables. I'm also a Giants fan, my favorite NFL player is the Giant's Eli Manning. I'm Filipino from the Philipines I will say something that will amaze you, "Ako I Pinoy." In English this means, "I am Filipino."

I'm going to ask you a question. When did you get a feeling that God wanted you to become a priest? I've got a problem with an older brother. How would you handle this problem?

I hope that you'll inspire other children to become priests. May the Lord be your protection.

Sincerely,
Raphael
5th grade
Blessed Trinity Catholic School

ARCHDIOCESE
OF
SAINT PAUL &
MINNEAPOLIS

Dear Raphael,

How wonderful that you are so young and have already lived in two countries and can speak another language. I always love meeting people from the Philippines — they have deep Catholic faith and great food (especially egg rolls).

Thanks for the question about when I got the feeling that God wanted me to become a priest. I first thought about being a priest when I was your age (and even younger), but I didn't know for sure until I was already out of college. I hope that you will give it some thought, particularly since you love listening to Jesus' stories and parables.

I hope that you are getting along with your older brother. Be patient with him. My younger brothers tell me that older brothers are bossy and tend to think that they know everything! That's not what I remember. We get along really well now.

+ Bernard A. Hebda

Grace

Convent of the Visitation School
Mendota Heights, MN

Fifth Grade

**"Why does it seem that miracles happen less often now?
Does it have something to do with people here today?"**

Dear Archbishop Hebda,

My name is Grace Keeley and I am a 5th grader at Visitation School in Mendota Heights. I live with my Mom, Dad and brother, Grant. I love to downhill ski in Big Sky, Montana and play basketball anytime, anywhere. (It's my favorite sport.) My favorite school subject is... well... I have a lot: art , science, language arts, spanish and gym. I am also very excited to be part of this project.

I liked learning about you, But as we were learning I found one question that was not yet asked or answered to me. People say that miracles are everywhere around me I just have to look. I am not a negative person, I try to look harder but I don't see anything. Why does it seem that miracles happen less often now? Does it have anything to do with people here today? Do you sometimes feel how I feel?

Thank you so much for taking the time out of your busy schedule to read my question. I am happy I had the opportunity to ask you my question.

Kindly,

Grace Keeley

Grace Keeley

14

ARCHDIOCESE
OF
SAINT PAUL &
MINNEAPOLIS

Dear Grace,

Thanks for your great questions. I am impressed that you have *five* favorite subjects and still find time to downhill ski and play basketball. I wasn't a very good skier, but I shared your love of basketball.

As for your question about miracles, I think that you are probably right that there are fewer obvious miracles these days. Jesus worked miracles so that people would believe in Him. Now that we already know that He rose from the dead (the greatest miracle), maybe other miracles would not be impressive enough to get us to believe. We tend to try to explain everything away.

I agree, however, with those who tell you that there are miracles happening all around you that will remind you that God is present in your life. I would encourage you to pray that you might have "eyes to see" them and "ears to hear" them. Just getting down one of your favorite slopes at Big Sky would be a miracle in my book.

+Bernd A. Hebda

William

St. Anne's Catholic School
Le Sueur, MN

Kindergarten

"How do priests get God to come down at Mass?"

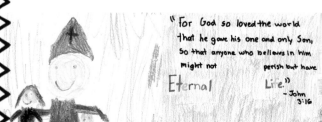

ARCHDIOCESE
OF
SAINT PAUL &
MINNEAPOLIS

Dear William,

      We are blessed because we don't have to convince God to come down — He already wants to be present to us in the bread and wine that become Jesus' Body and Blood.

      When He founded our Church, Jesus made sure that we would have priests who would be able to stand in his place and do just what He did at his Last Supper with the Apostles. He showed the Apostles what they would need to do (take the bread, bless it, break it and distribute it, and then do the same with the wine), and told them, "Do this in memory of me."

      Through the work of the Holy Spirit, what the priest does at Mass is what Jesus did at the Last Supper. What a blessing!

+Bernard A. Hebda

Abigail

Epiphany Catholic School
Coon Rapids, MN

First Grade

"Do you like dance?"

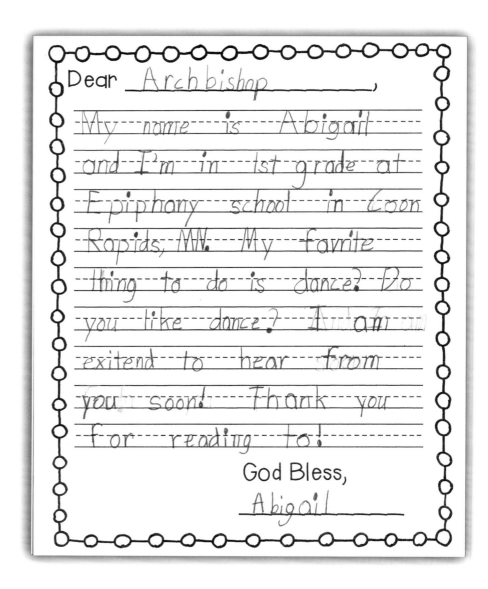

Dear _Archbishop_____,

My name is Abigail and I'm in 1st grade at Epiphany school in Coon Rapids, MN. My favrite thing to do is dance? Do you like dance? I am exitend to hear from you soon! Thank you for reading to!

God Bless,

_Abigail_____

Abigails favrite thing do is dan

Dear Abigail,

I bet that you are a much better dancer than I am. I don't dance so much anymore, but I used to love to dance before I became a priest. Dancing can be a great way to express what we are feeling when we hear great music. Once I became a priest, I limited myself to doing the Chicken Dance at weddings (and I have given even that up now that everyone has cameras on their cell phones).

We read in the Bible that King David, one of the greatest figures in the Old Testament, danced before the Ark of the Covenant to give glory to God. St. Teresa of Avila, the great Spanish saint, is reported to have once jumped onto a table and danced for her sisters while clicking castanets. Pope Francis loves the tango, and on his birthday a thousand couples came to St. Peter's Square in Rome to dance the tango for him. All in all, you are in very good company.

+Bernard A. Hebda

Riley

St. John the Baptist
Catholic School
Vermillion, MN

Fourth Grade

"Do you know all the names of the saints? Out of all the fun times in being an Archbishop, what was your favorite one?"

The Most Reverend Archbishop Bernard Hebda,

I'm Riley. I like to read the Bible. I'm in fourth grade and I am an altar server at St. Johns. My favorite story in the Bible is The Garden of Eden.

Archbishop, do you know all the names of the Saints? And another question is, out of all the fun times in being an Archbishop, what was your favorite one?

Thank you for leading our Archdiocese and I hope you can keep on leading us.

Respectfully yours in Christ,

Riley Ries

Dear Riley,

There are so many saints that I don't think that anyone could know all the names. I'm happy that on a good day I at least know the names of all the officially recognized saints who lived and served in the United States. If you become a saint (St. Riley), I promise that I will remember your name.

Of all the fun times that I have had as Archbishop, my favorite so far was the Mass of the Holy Spirit at CHS Field, with over 12,000 students from our Catholic schools. Were you there? The singing was great and the congregation energetic. I really felt the Holy Spirit there and hope that we will be able to gather like that again.

+Bernard A. Hebda

God's
Creation

Molly

St. John the Baptist
Catholic School
Savage, MN

Fourth Grade

"How do you feel God in your heart? What is your favorite ice cream?"

Dear Archbishop Hebda,

Hi, my name is Molly Wagner I am a 4th grader. My favorite subject is art because I love to draw. My favorite sport is soccer I always play forword. I'm happy I got an older kid bible this year! My favorite kind of color is black.

I want to ask you two questions. How do you feel God in your heart? What is your favorite kind of ice cream? I really hope you can write back.

I glad I could write a letter to you. Hopefuly you could be pope after Pope Francis.

love,
Molly ♥

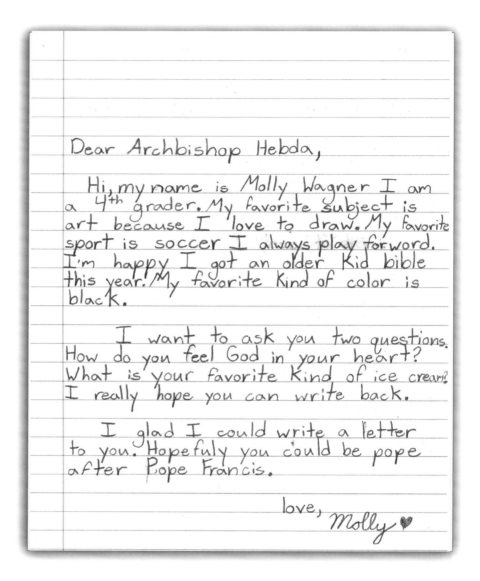

ARCHDIOCESE
OF
SAINT PAUL &
MINNEAPOLIS

Dear Molly,

I often feel God in my heart when I have done something good or whenever someone else has done something kind for me. I also feel Him in my heart when I hear a charming piece of music or see a beautiful painting or sculpture. There was a full moon last evening, and it really made me feel God in my heart as I saw it in the clear night sky above Target Field and the Minneapolis skyline.

As for ice cream flavors, you're going to think that I'm really boring. I love vanilla and strawberry! My favorite spot when I lived in Italy would make a wonderful almond and fig gelato. It sounds gross but was really delicious.

+Bernard A. Hebda

Michael

St. Therese Catholic School
Deephaven, MN

Fifth Grade

"Since you are the Archbishop, do you have your own house or do you live in a convent with other priests in it? Do you have to bring your staff with you?"

Dear Archbishop Hebda,

My name is Michael Sweeney. I'm a 5th grader at St. Therese school in Deephaven Minnesota. My teacher is Mrs. Goff, and there are 18 kids in my class including myself. I'm grateful that I'm getting the chance to write to you. I also love school and am very passionate about basketball too.

I have a few questions for you that I hope you can help answer. My first question is, since you are the archbishop do you have your own house or do you live in a convent with other priests in it? Secondly, when you are in public, do you have to bring your staff with you because I think that would be a hassle. Also, I was wondering if Archbishops have the same system for saying the mass. I know that each priest says the mass differently, but do Archbishops have to do something that school preists don't have to do?

Dear Michael,

I live with three other priests in the rectory at the Cathedral in Saint Paul. I am very grateful that they do not complain that they can hear my snoring through the walls.

As for my staff, I will let you in on a secret: it's not a hassle to bring it because it is very light and breaks down into four pieces. I usually ask the altar servers to put it together for me.

The Mass is pretty much the same whether it is celebrated by an Archbishop or by a priest. What I wear is a little different than what a priest wears, but otherwise the Mass is the same. My friends tell me, however, that my homilies are longer now that I am an Archbishop.

+Bernard A. Hebda

Fiona

Holy Name of Jesus
Catholic School
Wayzata, MN

Fourth Grade

"I would like to ask you why women have to be nuns, why can't they be priests?"

Hello Archbishop Hebda,

Hi! I'm Fiona Foster. I am 10 years old and I go to Holy Name of Jesus catholic school. It is a very great school and I love my teacher, Mrs.Doblar. I heard that you came to visit on February 14th!
I would like to ask you why women have to be nuns, why can't they be priests? I would like to be a priest. People could just call me 'Sister Fiona (or Sister Foster)'. I would love to know the answer.

Thank you for reading my letter! I really appreciate it!

Love, and great wishes,
Fiona
Fiona

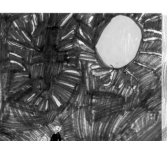

ARCHDIOCESE
OF
SAINT PAUL &
MINNEAPOLIS

Dear Fiona,

I think that is one of those questions we are going to have to wait and ask Jesus about, for a complete answer. The Church ordains only men to be priests because that is what Jesus did. We are imitating him. Jesus had deep friendships with women (He appeared first to Mary Magdalene after His Resurrection) and surely knew that some of them were far stronger and holier than the Apostles that He chose (no one was holier than Jesus' mother, Mary), but He nonetheless chose 12 men to be the first priests and the Church has followed that example ever since. That doesn't mean that men are better than women or that women cannot exercise real leadership in the Church. In our Archdiocese, I thank God for the great work that is being accomplished by faithful Catholic women at the archdiocesan and parish levels. I hope that you will find lots of opportunities for using the gifts that God has given you. We need great leaders.

If you read the lives of the great women saints, I am sure that you will have lots of ideas for how God might be calling you to be a leader in His Church.

+Bernard A. Hebda

Henry

St. Jude of the Lake
Catholic School
Mahtomedi, MN

Fifth Grade

"How or in what way can we love our enemies? What are your suggestions?"

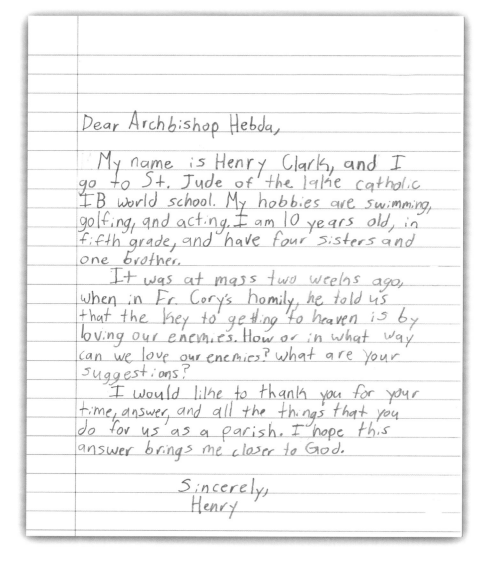

Dear Archbishop Hebda,

My name is Henry Clark, and I go to St. Jude of the lake catholic IB world school. My hobbies are swimming, golfing, and acting. I am 10 years old, in fifth grade, and have four sisters and one brother.

It was at mass two weeks ago, when in Fr. Cory's homily, he told us that the key to getting to heaven is by loving our enemies. How or in what way can we love our enemies? what are your suggestions?

I would like to thank you for your time, answer, and all the things that you do for us as a parish. I hope this answer brings me closer to God.

Sincerely,
Henry

Dear Henry,

I was happy to hear that you listen so closely to Father Cory's homilies. You have a great pastor, who can teach you lots of wonderful things.

I think the best way for us to love our enemies is to try to understand them and to see them as God sees them. It's much easier to love them if we remember that they are God's sons and daughters too. I also think that it is easier to love them when we remember that we're not perfect and that we sometimes make mistakes and do annoying things too.

+Bernard A. Hebda

Tim

St. Michael Catholic School
Saint Michael, MN

First Grade

**"Should I be a priest
because I love God?"**

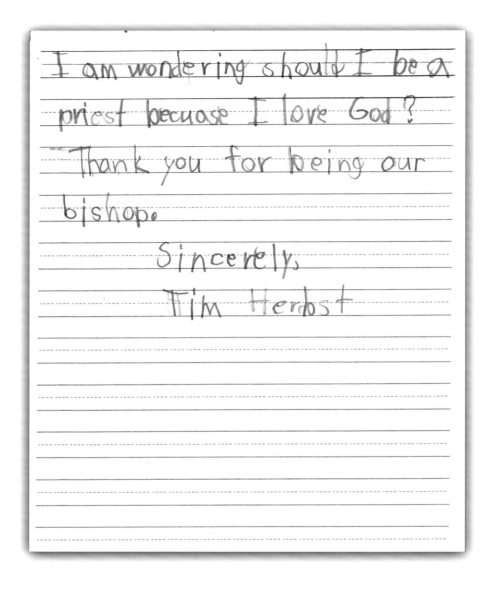

I am wondering should I be a priest becuase I love God? Thank you for being our bishop.

Sincerely,
Tim Herbst

ARCHDIOCESE
OF
SAINT PAUL &
MINNEAPOLIS

Dear Tim,

You still have lots of time to decide whether you should become a priest . . . but I sure am glad that you are thinking about it. While loving God is a big part of being a priest, loving God can also be a big part of being a great dad and husband.

I was thrilled to learn that religion is already one of your favorite subjects and really happy to hear that you read the Bible every night. Because of your love for God, I am confident that you will hear Him when He lets you know what He wants you to do with your life. Keep reading and learning about God and His Church, do your best to lead a good life and remember to speak to God in prayer. If you do those things, God will surely take care of the rest.

+Bernard A. Hebda

Alexa

St. Elizabeth Ann Seton
Catholic School
Hastings, MN

Fourth Grade

"I have always had a hard time putting God above all things. Do you have any advice for me?"

Dear Arch Bishop Hebda,

    I am Alexa Loritz. I go to school at Saint Elizabeth Ann Seton Catholic School in Hastings Minasota. I love to play soccer and read books. My favorite books are the Harry Potter books.

    I have always had trouble putting God above addictive things such as T.V., reading, and going outdoors. Do you have any advice for me? It feels like God and the devil are playing tug-of-war with me, like I am human string cheese! It has botherd me for years. Please pray for me.

    Thank you for reading my letter, and I hope you have a good rest of your day!

Sincerily,
Alexa L

34

Dear Alexa,

I just met your grandmother and grandfather at the parish festival at St. John Neumann, and I told them that I loved your question and what you said about sometimes feeling like string cheese, being pulled in one direction by God and the other by the Devil.

My advice for learning how to put God first in your life (even before TV!) is to take time each day to count your blessings, to remember just how God has blessed you in the course of the day. I usually do that just before I go to bed. I think back to everything I did that day and look for signs that God was present. It's a way that I remember just how much God loves us and how active He is in my life. When I see that, I realize that He deserves to be the most important person in my life. I then ask Him to help me put Him first. I hope that works for you too (before the string cheese snaps).

+Bernard A. Hebda

Allison

St. John the Baptist
Catholic School
Vermillion, MN

Third Grade

"Do Archbishops have terms like Presidents or Popes? Do Archbishops die like people?"

Dear Archbishop,

Hi, I'm Allison, I like hockey, I love my family, I have a mom and a dad, and a brother. I have a favorite Bible sentence, it is: Give thanks to the lord, for his love endures forever. (Palm 118:1)

I also have 2 questions for you, Number 1. Do Archbishops have terms like Presidents or Popes? Number 2, Do Archbishops die like people?

Thank you Archbishop for being a good leader, thank you for blessing us, Thank you for coming to our church last year.

Your Friend, Allison - grade 3

St. John the Baptist School Vermillion, Mn

ARCHDIOCESE
OF
SAINT PAUL &
MINNEAPOLIS

Dear Allison,

I am happy that you already have a favorite Bible verse (Psalm 118:1) and have to tell you that it is one of my favorites as well ("Give thanks to the Lord, for his love endures forever").

You can be thankful that I won't be your Archbishop forever. While we don't have terms like the president, we do have to offer to retire when we reach the age of 75 (another 17 years for me — way longer than a president can serve).

As for your question about whether Archbishops die like people, I can happily tell you that WE ARE PEOPLE! I love to go out to Calvary Cemetery in Saint Paul, where the first Archbishop of our diocese, Archbishop Ireland, is buried. It is a peaceful place to think and pray, and it reminds me that we never know how much time the Lord will give us, so we better make good use of each day.

+Bernard A. Hebda

Logan

St. Croix Catholic School
Stillwater, MN

Fourth Grade

"Have you ever met the Pope? Do you think that every Pope has a piece of the cross? If you could meet anybody from history, who would it be?"

Logan

Dear Archbishop Hebda,
My name's Logan I come from a catholic school. I have some questions to ask you. Have you ever met the Pope? Do you think every Pope has a big piece of the cross? If you could meet anybody from history who would it be? Thank you for giving me the priviledge to write to you.

Sincerely,
Logan

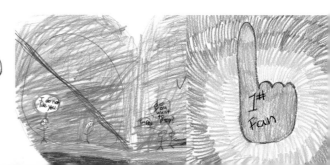

Dear Logan,

I have met Pope Francis four times (three times in Rome and once in the United States) and enjoyed every visit. I found him to be very kind and very encouraging. I think that it would be great if he would come to Minnesota. I bet that he has never been ice fishing.

I don't know if every Pope personally has a "big piece of the cross," but I know that they have one in the big church right next to where the Pope lives (St. Peter's in Rome). They put it out for people to see on the fifth Sunday of Lent.

As for a person from history who I would like to meet, I would love to have the chance to speak with St. Philip Neri. He was a great priest and role model for young people. I would love to know a little more about what made him so joyful.

+Bernard A. Hebda

Avery

Saint Wenceslaus
Catholic School
New Prague, MN

Fourth Grade

**"Have you ever seen
God in other people,
and if so, how?"**

Dear Archbishop Bernard Hebda,
    I am a fourth grader at Saint Wenceslaus School in New Prague. My favorite subject is religon. I love to pray and go to mass. My favorite Saint is Saint Sebastion. My favorite Gospel story is the Prodigal Son just like yours. I love to dream big.

    I was wondering if you have ever seen God in other people, and if so, how?

    Thank you for taking time out of your day to read all the letters we have written. Thank you for being a great role model. You are a follower of Jesus, and that is a great thing. Thank you for standing outside of the box. I would love to be like you. Prayers are coming your way.

Sincerely,

Avery Gullickson

ARCHDIOCESE
OF
SAINT PAUL &
MINNEAPOLIS

Dear Avery,

I feel really blessed that I often catch glimpses of God in other people. One of the best parts of being Archbishop is that I often get to meet with people who tell me about their great work in the Church. As I listen to their stories, I often recognize Jesus in their compassion, or God the Father in their patience or the Holy Spirit in their joy.

You mentioned that you share my love for the story of the Prodigal Son. I bet that if we could meet the father in that story, we would catch a glimpse of God in him, especially in his willingness to forgive, love and embrace his runaway son.

Mother Teresa would challenge her sisters to look for Jesus "in the distressing disguise of the poor." Let's pray for the grace to be able to recognize Jesus in our midst when He is passing by.

+Bernard A. Hebda

Callan

St. Thomas More
Catholic School
Saint Paul, MN

Kindergarten

"Why do you wear both hats?"

Dear Archbishop Hebda,

My name is Callan Walsh and I am a Kindergartener at St. Thomas More School in St. Paul. Guess what... I am learning to read! I can read a whole book by myself.

In September, we watched the all-school Mass at the Saints stadium in our auditorium at school. I saw you wearing the tall white hat (mitre) and when you took it off, you had on a red hat (zucchetto). Why do you wear both hats?

Thank you for reading my letter.

Callan

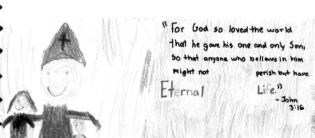

Dear Callan,

That's a question I have been asking for years. Wearing two hats makes me really hot most of the time. The pointy white hat is called a mitre, and it's something that any bishop would wear. The flaps in the back are leftovers from the days when bishops would ride horses; they would tie the flaps under their chin so that the miter would not fall off. My mom used to say that a bishop had to wear the pointy hat so that the whole congregation would know if he started to nod off.

The skullcap, called a zucchetto, comes in different colors and indicates the priest's rank: priests can wear black, bishops and Archbishops wear purple, cardinals wear red and the Pope wears white. Zucchetto means "little pumpkin" in Italian. If you look at it up close, it looks like the top piece of a jack-o'-lantern (even with a little stem).

+Bernard A. Hebda

Kallie

Saint Wenceslaus
Catholic School
New Prague, MN

First Grade

"Are you ever scared?"

Dear Archbishop Hebda
My name is Kallie.
I am 6 years old. I go to
St. Wenceslaus School.
I am in 1st grade. I like
Easter.
This is my question for
you: Are you ever scared?
Thank you for your
service.
From, Kallie Schiell

ARCHDIOCESE
OF
SAINT PAUL &
MINNEAPOLIS

Dear Kallie,

I think that we all get scared sometimes. I don't like driving on ice, my voice gets very high whenever I see alligators while visiting my family in Florida and I often start to sweat when I have to speak before really large crowds outside of church. For me, those fears have all led me to pray.

Jesus promises us that He will be with us always and that the Holy Spirit will give us the right words to say. I always need to remind myself of those things. I once read that there are 365 places in the Bible where people are told to "be not afraid" — one for every day of the year. I never counted them myself, but I know that is an important part of God's message for us.

+Bernard A. Hebda

Ethan

St. Stephen's Catholic School
Anoka, MN

Fourth Grade

"I want to know why and how you became a priest."

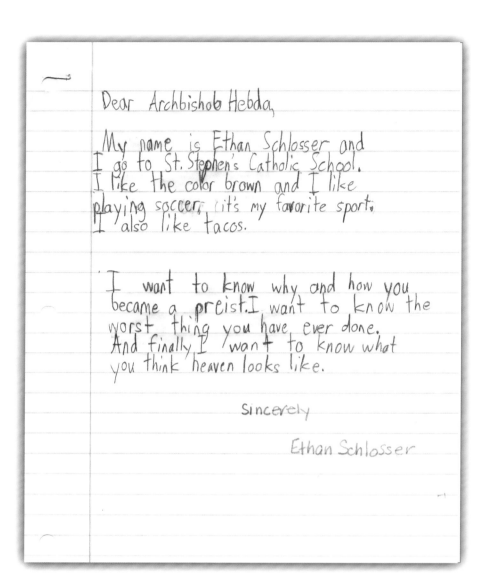

Dear Archbishob Hebda,

My name is Ethan Schlosser and I go to St. Stephen's Catholic School. I like the color brown and I like playing soccer, it's my favorite sport, I also like tacos.

I want to know why and how you became a preist. I want to know the worst thing you have ever done. And finally I want to know what you think heaven looks like.

Sincerely

Ethan Schlosser

ARCHDIOCESE
OF
SAINT PAUL &
MINNEAPOLIS

Dear Ethan,

Thank you for your questions. Once I read that you like tacos, I knew that you would ask good questions.

I became a priest because I believed that was part of God's plan for me. While it surprised me that God would choose me (I had two brothers who seemed like they would have been better choices), I became convinced that He was indeed calling me, and I felt that I needed to say "yes."

Like most priests, I prepared for priesthood by entering the seminary. I went first to a seminary in Pittsburgh, where I studied philosophy (the study of life's "big questions"), and then to a seminary in Rome, where I studied theology (which focused on God and His Church). While in the seminary, we also learn more about prayer and about how to be good shepherds. I enjoyed my years in seminary very much. Here in the Twin Cities, we have two excellent seminaries: one for men in college and the other for men who have already graduated from college.

+Bernard A. Hebda

Morgan

St. Thomas More
Catholic School
Saint Paul, MN

Kindergarten

**"How old are you?
Do you wear that big cross
all the time?"**

Dear Archbishop Hebda,

My name is Morgan Houser and I am a Kindergartener at St. Thomas More School in St. Paul. I like to go to school and learn new things. My favorite things in school are Superkids (reading program) and religion. I also love to make things using the craft box.

I am 6 years old, how old are you? Sometimes my mom lets me wear a necklace to school. You have a really big cross necklace. Do you wear that big cross all the time? I think it is pretty.

Thank you for reading my letter.

Love,

Morgan

ARCHDIOCESE
OF
SAINT PAUL &
MINNEAPOLIS

Dear Morgan,

I am almost 10 times older than you. I turned 58 on September 3rd.

I am surprised that you remembered my cross. I guess that it is a little on the big side. It was a gift from some friends when I was named a bishop, and I wear it every day (but not to bed and not when I go swimming). It is supposed to remind me and those who see it of Jesus' great love. I bet that you could make a cross like mine by using your craft box.

I was happy to hear that you really enjoy the Superkids reading program at St. Thomas More School. You must be much smarter than I am. I didn't learn how to read until I was in the first grade.

+Bernard A. Hebda

Luke

All Saints Catholic School
Lakeville, MN

Kindergarten

**"When you were little
did you like to jump
in mud puddles?"**

Dear <u>Archbishop Hebda</u>,

<u>When you were little did you</u>
<u>like to jump in mud puddles?</u>
<u>I lost my rain boots so I</u>
<u>have to stay inside when it</u>
<u>rains.</u>

Love,

<u>LUKE</u>

ARCHDIOCESE
OF
SAINT PAUL &
MINNEAPOLIS

Dear Luke,

Who told you that I used to jump in mud puddles? I never met a mud puddle that I didn't like. As a kid, I seemed to be attracted to anything involving dirt.

I am sorry to hear that you lost your rain boots. I haven't lost my boots, but I have lost plenty of other things. I learned when I was your age that St. Anthony is the saint who helps people to find things that are lost. I pray to him all the time. I call on him for help so often that I should have him on speed dial. I hope that he helps you as he has helped me.

+ Bernard A. Hebda

Lily

St. John Catholic School
of Little Canada
Little Canada, MN

Kindergarten

**"Can God see through
your heart?"**

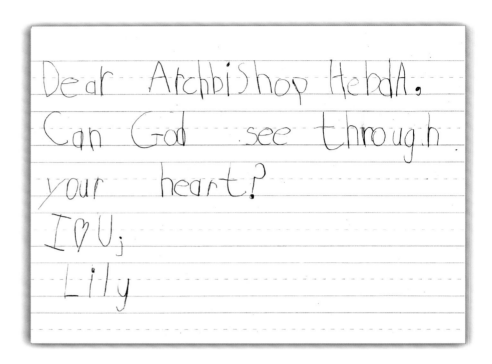

Dear Archbishop Hebda,
Can God see through
your heart?
I ♥ U,
Lily

Dear Lily,

God made us and knows everything about us. We read in the Bible that He even knows when we sit and when we stand, that He knows what we are going to say even before the words are formed on our tongue. That's how much He loves us. He sees right through to our heart.

Because God already knows everything about us, we can be totally honest with Him and speak to Him about the things in our heart. Knowing that God sees everything that we do, I try to live in a way that would make Him smile (even when I make silly mistakes).

Carter

St. Dominic Catholic School
Northfield, MN

Third Grade

"Have you ever felt the Holy Spirit? How do I love someone who has hurt me? How do I get closer to God?"

Dear Archbishop Hebda,

My name is Carter Simon

I am in ___3___ grade at St. Dominic School.

These are things I like to do: ~~Play~~ Street hockey, Play football, golf, and basketball.

Here is something you did not know about me:
I play hockey I live next to a park.

I enjoyed learning about you from my teacher.

Here is my question for you: Have you ever felt the Holy Spirit? How do I love someone who has hurt me? How do I get closer to God?

I think this is a fun way to get to know you better.

Blessings to you,

Carter

ARCHDIOCESE
OF
SAINT PAUL &
MINNEAPOLIS

Dear Carter,

I feel blessed that I often feel the Holy Spirit. At times, the feeling is so strong that even tears of joy fill my eyes. That sometimes embarrasses me — but I am grateful for the strong reminder of the closeness of the Holy Spirit.

When we invite the Holy Spirit into our lives, amazing things happen. One of the Holy Spirit's jobs is to help us to pray, to draw us closer to God. When we ask for help in that area, the Holy Spirit never lets us down. It's the Holy Spirit, moreover, who can help us love someone who has hurt us. Sometimes the Holy Spirit does that by reminding us of the times that we ourselves have hurt others and needed love and forgiveness. On other occasions, the Holy Spirit might give us insights into what might have led the other person to hurt us, and that can sometimes help us to love them more. You never know what is going to happen when you let the Holy Spirit into your heart.

Hannah

St. Helena's Catholic School
Minneapolis, MN

First Grade

"How did they think of churches? Because I want to build a church."

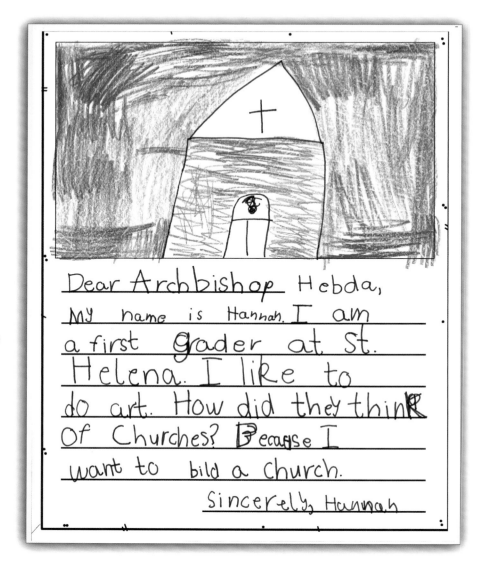

Dear Archbishop Hebda,
My name is Hannah. I am a first grader at St. Helena. I like to do art. How did they think Of Churches? Because I want to bild a church.
Sincerely, Hannah

ARCHDIOCESE OF **SAINT PAUL & MINNEAPOLIS**

Dear Hannah,

Thank you for your question. It is one that I have asked many times myself, particularly when I sit in the many beautiful churches in our Archdiocese. Not only are they beautiful to the eye, but they also teach us about our faith. Have you ever noticed that many churches are in the shape of a cross, while many others look like upside-down boats (remember the story about how Jesus calmed the seas when He was in a boat?). I particularly love stained glass windows that teach us about the life of Jesus or Mary or of one of the saints. Sometimes they even teach us about Baptism, Holy Communion and the other sacraments.

I sure hope that you will have a chance to fulfill your dream of building a church. I hope that it will be a church as beautiful as the one that you go to, St. Helena's. That would be a great way to use your talents to give glory to God.

+Bernard A. Hebda

Dominic

Saint Agnes Catholic School
Saint Paul, MN

Second Grade

"Have you ever seen an animal while saying Mass? What was it? Was anyone scared?"

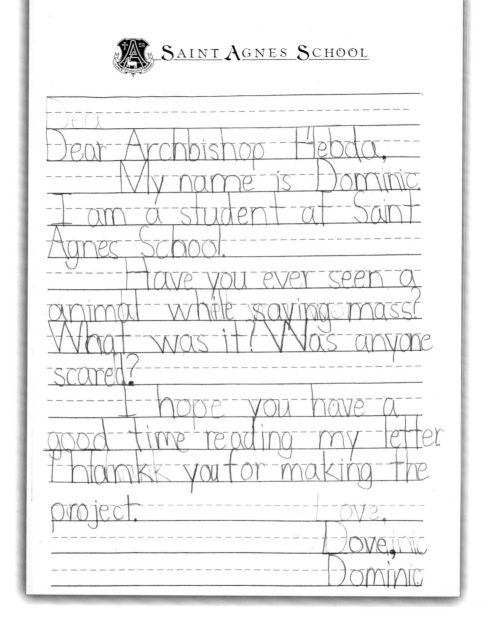

SAINT AGNES SCHOOL

Dear

Dear Archbishop Hebda,
My name is Dominic.
I am a student at Saint
Agnes School.
Have you ever seen a
animal while saying mass?
What was it? Was anyone
scared?
I hope you have a
good time reading my letter
Thankk you for making the
project.
Love,
Dove,inic
Dominic

"For God so loved the world that he gave his one and only Son, so that anyone who believes in him might not perish but have Eternal Life." ~ John 3:16

Youre on the ROAD!!!!

Faith Hope

ARCHDIOCESE
OF
SAINT PAUL &
MINNEAPOLIS

Dear Dominic,

I have fond memories of celebrating Mass for the Knights of Columbus when a bat kept trying to hide in their feathered hats! The congregation gasped with each dive of the bat. I don't think that anyone remembered my homily that day.

I have also had dogs and cats wander into church while I was celebrating Mass, as well as an occasional pigeon, but no one was scared.

When I lived in Italy, I had Mass in the church in Gubbio, where they buried the famous wolf that St. Francis tamed — that was a little strange but not frightening. I have also had Mass where St. Francis used to preach to the birds and where St. Anthony preached to the fish.

+Bernard A. Hebda

Abby

Nativity of Our Lord
Catholic School
Saint Paul, MN

First Grade

"When you are lonely, does God guide you?"

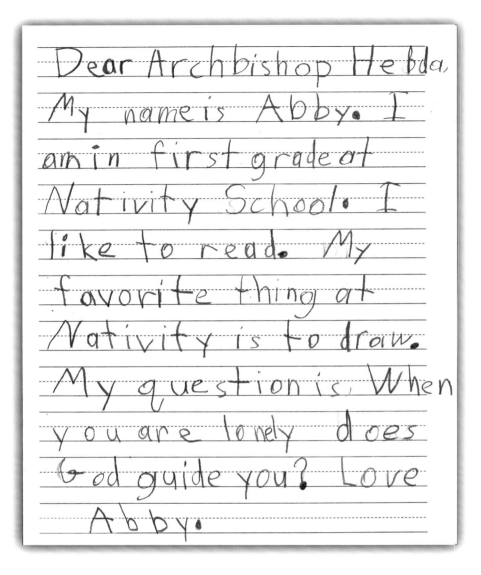

Dear Archbishop Hebda,
My name is Abby. I am in first grade at Nativity School. I like to read. My favorite thing at Nativity is to draw. My question is When you are lonely does God guide you? Love Abby.

Abigails favrite thing do is draw

ARCHDIOCESE
OF
SAINT PAUL &
MINNEAPOLIS

Dear Abby,

Thanks for your question. I absolutely go to the Lord for help when I am lonely, and He has never let me down. Before I was a priest, I was sent to Rome for seminary and was not able to come home to see my family and friends for two years, and it was before the invention of Skype and Facetime. I was really homesick, but the more that I turned to the Lord, the more I came to realize that I was never really alone, that He was always with me to strengthen and guide me. It was a great lesson.

Any time that I am really lonely, I find my way to our little chapel and spend some time in prayer, remembering all that God has done for me, and the loneliness seems to go away. God is so good.

+Bernard A. Hebda

Tyson

St. Helena's Catholic School
Minneapolis, MN

First Grade

"Why do angels glow?"

Dear Archbishop Nienstedt,

Why do angels glow? From, Tyson

www.teaching-with-style.com

Dear Tyson,

You must be very special if you know that angels glow. I have never yet been blessed to see an angel. I would not be surprised, however, to learn that they glow, since they must always be so happy to be in the presence of God. They beam with joy. I know that artists try to capture that joy by giving angels halos that surround their head. To show that angels are often sent on missions and are always in motion, artists usually paint them with wings.

I don't know about you, but I would need really strong wings to get me from place to place. I would particularly love to have wings when our Minnesota roads are under construction.

+Bernard A. Hebda

God's
Creation

Hailey

Good Shepherd Catholic School
Golden Valley, MN

Fourth Grade

**"Will everyone go to heaven?
Will I ever see her [my
deceased cousin] again?"**

Dear Archbishop Hebda,
    I am 10 years old. My name is Hailey. I go to Good Shepherd School. I am the oldest in my family. I have one sibling in secound grade.
    I have been wondering ever since my cousin/best friend died. Will everyone go to heaven? And will I ever see her again?
    Thank you for giving me the opportunity to write to you. This was fun.

From,
Hailey

Good Shepherd
Golden Valley

ARCHDIOCESE
OF
SAINT PAUL &
MINNEAPOLIS

Dear Hailey,

Great question! I think that it is God's desire that we would all go to heaven. The fact that He would send us His beloved son, Jesus, is for me the proof of that desire. He sent us Jesus to give us the possibility of going to heaven. God doesn't force us to go to heaven and gives us all kinds of choices in life. If we choose to love God and want to go to heaven, I am confident that God will find a place for us there.

No one knows for sure what heaven is like, but we believe that every longing in our hearts is satisfied there. With that in mind, I would guess that there will be many loving family reunions there.

+Bernard A. Hebda

Henry

Nativity of Our Lord
Catholic School
Saint Paul, MN

Kindergarten

**"How do you make the
world better?"**

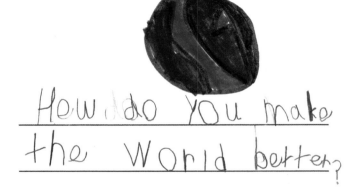

Dear Archbishop Hebda,

How do you make
the World better?

Love,

Henry

ARCHDIOCESE
— OF —
SAINT PAUL &
MINNEAPOLIS

Dear Henry,

    I love your question. To make the world better, we need to use the gifts that God has given to each one of us. None of us can do it on our own, but we can do great things if we put our heads and hearts together. Just think about the talents of all the wonderful students at your school. I hope that you are all dreaming big.

+Bernard A. Hebda

Jessica

Providence Academy
Plymouth, MN

Third Grade

"What will the end of the world be like? My brother thinks it will be a zombie apocalypse and my teacher thinks that Jesus and all of the saints will come down."

Dear Archbiship Hebda

My name is Jessica Shore I am a student at Providence Academy, I relly relly relly want to be a saint when I grow up, Every day at school we have chapel time,

One thing that I always wanted to know was what will the end of the world be like? My brother thinks it will be a zombe apoclypse and my teacher Mr.Dudley thinks that Jesus and all of the saints will come down form Heaven and bring us up to Heaven,

ARCHDIOCESE
OF
SAINT PAUL &
MINNEAPOLIS

Dear Jessica,

Zombie apocalypse? Really? Tell your brother that I think he watches too many movies.

We Catholics do believe that Jesus will come again — and when He comes, He will really raise up the bodies of the dead. That shouldn't, however, be something that makes us afraid (like a zombie apocalypse) but something that gives us hope. St. Paul tells us that Jesus is going to give new form to our lowly bodies so that they conform to His glorious Body. I can hardly wait.

+Bernard A. Hebda

Rafael

St. Helena's Catholic School
Minneapolis, MN

First Grade

**"Are you friends
with saints?"**

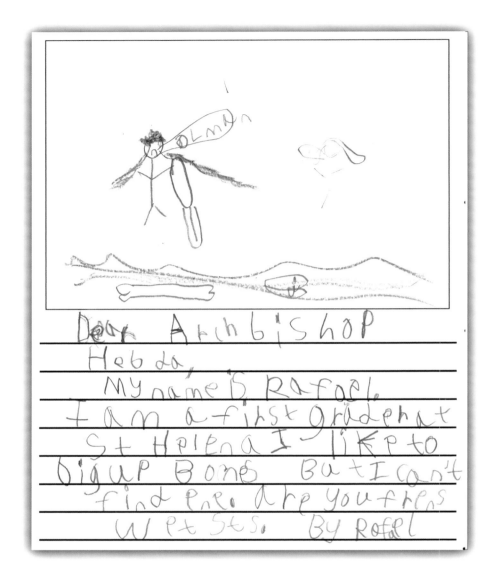

Dear Archbishop Hebda,
My name is Rafael. I am a first grade at St Helena I like to dig up Bones But I can't find ene. Are you freds wet sts. By Rafael

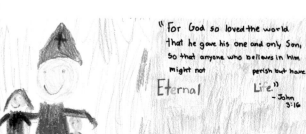

"For God so loved the world that he gave his one and only Son, So that anyone who believes in him might not perish but have Eternal Life." - John 3:16

You're on the ROAD!!!

Faith   Hope

ARCHDIOCESE
OF
SAINT PAUL &
MINNEAPOLIS

Dear Rafael,

I am inspired by many of the saints and always try to learn more about them. My favorite saints have been St. Bernard and St. Anthony (because I am named for them) and St. Philip Neri, who was so joyful in his service of the Lord. Now that I am the Archbishop in Saint Paul, I am trying to grow in my friendship with our patron saint, St. Paul, who gave his life to spreading the Good News of Jesus. We honor the saints because they were able to show in their lives that they were friends of Jesus. Any friend of Jesus has to be a friend of mine.

I bet that you, as someone who likes to dig up bones, would love to learn about relics. We feel a special closeness to a saint when we are close to his or her bones — we call those bones "relics" because the bones are what "remains" of the saint on earth after they have died and gone to heaven (the word "relic" comes from the Latin word for "remains").

There are special patron saints for different activities, usually because the saint was connected in some way to that activity. St. Hubert, for example, is the patron saint of hunters, while St. Cecilia is the patron saint of musicians. Perhaps you can someday be the patron saint of bone hunters.

+Bernd A. Hebda

Ella

Our Lady of the Lake
Catholic School
Mound, MN

Second Grade

"Have you ever wanted to explode with kindness but can't? Or ever wonder why nobody's perfect?"

Dear Archbishop Hebda,

My name is Ella I go to school at Our Lady of the Lake in mound.I am in second grade.
At school my favorite subject is Art because you get to be creative.
I remember Fr. Tony once saying a Saint is a sinner who keeps on trying.

My question for you is have you ever wanted to explode with kindness but can't?
Or ever wonder why nobody's perfect?

Thank you for being our Archbishop. You have been a great Archbishop

Love,
Ella.

ARCHDIOCESE
OF
SAINT PAUL &
MINNEAPOLIS

Dear Ella,

What an interesting question! There are plenty of times when I wish that I could be more kind, more patient and more understanding, but I don't ever remember being ready to explode with kindness. I am guessing that you have had that experience. I would love to be with someone when that happened, and I can imagine that it would be like being rained upon with goodness. Sounds pretty great! I think that if I ever wanted to explode with kindness, I would pray that God would show me the best way to express what was inside me.

I am guessing that those who encountered Jesus when He walked the earth would have experienced explosions of His kindness, His forgiveness, and His compassion. I think about Zaccheus, Mary Magdalene and Matthew. They must have been overwhelmed by Jesus' kindness.

I have a feeling that our idea of "perfect" is quite different from God's. God, in his perfection, creates us just as He intends. I should not think of my height or my uncontrollable hair as being imperfections if that's how God lovingly created me. I sometimes think that God made us with our shortcomings so that we would need others and form communities. If we were all "perfect," the temptation would be to think that we didn't need anyone else, not even God.

+Bernard A. Hebda

Gianmarco

Highland Catholic School
Saint Paul, MN

Fourth Grade

"What do you think is your favorite prayer? Do you normally pray before you go to bed and at meals?"

Dear Archbishop Hebda,

   My name is Gianmarco Veglia. I go to Highland Catholic School, and I'm in 4th grade. I play hockey and soccer, and I like to read, play sports, and play with my friends. I am 10 years old, and I have a brother and a sister who are both older than me. I have grandparents, cousins, uncles, and aunts in Italy and in Massachusetts.

   I was wondering why you chose to be an Archbishop? What do you think is your favorite prayer? If you do have a favorite prayer, why is it your favorite? Do you normally pray before you go to bed and at meals?

   Thank you for leading the mass at CHS field! I hope you can come visit our school soon.

Sincerely,
Gianmarco

Gianmarco

Dear Gianmarco,

I was blessed with great parents, who made sure that we would always pray before meals and pray before going to bed, and I continue to rely on that foundation. Those moments of prayer are wonderful opportunities for remembering what God has done for us.

My favorite prayer is the "Our Father" because it is the prayer that Jesus taught to His disciples when they asked Him to teach them how to pray. I often try to imagine that I am praying it along with Jesus as He teaches it to me.

I also really like the prayers, such as the "Hail Mary" and the "Memorare," that remind us that we can turn to the Blessed Virgin Mary for help as well. She is a mother who loves us and never lets us down.

+Bernard A. Hebda

Claire

St. Peter Catholic School
North Saint Paul, MN

Fifth Grade

"Why would such a loving, kind God allow someone to suffer that great?"

Dear Archbishop Hebda,

Hello! My name is Claire Huss, I'm in 5th grade and am 11 years old! It is truly an honor to write to you, and I'm thankful for your time. ~~Now~~ Now, a little about myself.

I enjoy writing, reading, volleyball, soccer, and softball. I am learning Spanish, and writing a story.

Oh right, my question. So, last month, a kid in my class' mother died due to Alhzimers Disease, and we've been having a difficult time as a class. It's hard to even imagine a loss that great. My question is, why would such a loving, kind, God allow someone to suffer that great? I'm sure you must get this question often, but I'd like answer.

Thank you so much,

Claire Huss

Dear Claire,

I believe that it is God's desire that we would all be with Him one day in heaven, where's there no suffering. The best that I can figure out is that God allows suffering because it in some way helps us to get there. I was sorry to hear about your classmate's mother and know that sickness and the loss of a parent is very painful for a family. I know from experience, however, that those moments of pain can also be times when we reach out to God in a new way, when we can grow closer to Him, when we see things in a new way.

We are blessed that we have a God who understands our pain. The Bible tells us, for example, that Jesus wept when He heard about the death of His friend, Lazarus. We also know that Jesus Himself embraced the pain of the Cross, recognizing that it would bring about something far greater than His pain.

How beautiful that a very difficult experience in your classmate's life would make your heart grow more like Jesus', filled with compassion. I suspect that's one of the ways that God prepares you for heaven.

+Bernard A. Hebda

Landon

Sacred Heart Catholic School
Robbinsdale, MN

Fifth Grade

"In what ways have you run into some difficult moments and why were they so difficult?"

Dear Archbishop Hebda,

Hello my name is Landon. This might not be the best letter you've seen but I will indeed try my best. Thank you for everything. For teaching others telling about God and what he did for us. I hope you have fun doing it. And I as a citizen must respect all what you have done for many different schools. I go to school at Robbinsdale Sacred Heart Catholic School. It's fun learning here and going to mass every Friday but sadly today is Monday and I have to go to a surgery so I can't attend school on Wednesday, Thursday, or Friday.

I'm a little sad I have too miss Ash Wednesday and mass but this surgery is important to me so I don't get bullied it's not fun. In what ways have you ran into some difficult moments and why were they so difficult? This is important to me so I know what my future self will be like, and what difficult times will I have? I know this is a little long but hope you enjoyed and it will be an honor to be able to meet you in real life. But anyway have an amazing year Archbishop!

Sincerely,
Your friend Landon
5th Grader
Sacred Heart Catholic School
Robbinsdale

ARCHDIOCESE
OF
SAINT PAUL &
MINNEAPOLIS

Dear Landon,

     Now that you are in fifth grade, you probably realize that all of us have difficult times. That is true for me as well. I can remember that it felt like my heart was breaking four years ago, when I was transferred from Michigan to New Jersey. I really loved the people in my diocese in Northern Michigan, and it was very hard to leave them. When we open our hearts to love others, it can be painful when we have to be separated.

     In time, I came to love the people that I met in New Jersey as well, and that has been my experience in Minnesota too. It is amazing how God can use those difficult moments to make us stronger and to help us to trust more in Him.

+Bernd A. Hebda

Olivia

St. Pascal Baylon Catholic School
Saint Paul, MN

Fifth Grade

"Have you ever witnessed a miracle and what was it? Do you have any fears about being a bishop?"

Dear, Archbishop Hebda,

My name is Olivia Slater I'm a 5th grader at St. Pascal's. I'm a dancer at Yackel Dance. My favorite class is gym because there are fun activities to do, such as, Volleyball and Hockey.

We are learning about sacrements this year in school. Which made me thinking, have you ever witnessed a miracle, and what was it? Also being a bishop is a hard job. Do you have any fears about being a Bishop? We are praying for you and thank you for your work.

Sincerely,
Olivia Slater

ARCHDIOCESE — OF — **SAINT PAUL & MINNEAPOLIS**

Dear Olivia,

I was so happy to hear that you pray for me. Thanks. I don't have any fears about being a bishop, but I am well aware that I need lots of help and lots of prayers if I am going to be a good leader for this local Church. The Archdiocese has a beautiful history, and I would not ever want to do anything that would give anyone reason to leave the Church or lose faith in Jesus' promise that He will be with His Church always, until the end of time.

As for miracles, I believe that I see miracles all the time. The best part of being a priest is that we often get to see how the Holy Spirit works in the lives of God's people. Every time God manages to enter a hard heart, that's a miracle in my book. Every time He inspires someone to find hope in a difficult situation, that's a miracle too.

We have to help each other recognize the amazing things that God does for us every day. I have seen people make amazing recoveries from illness; sometimes it's because they met just the right doctor, or the doctor tried just the right option or they arrived at the hospital in the nick of time. Some would see these as mere coincidences, but I believe they are the work of God and often the answer to prayers.

+Bernard A. Hebda

Myles

St. Joseph Catholic School
Waconia, MN

Fourth Grade

"How hard is it to be a priest? How did you know that God wanted you to be a priest?"

Dear Archbishop Hebda,

My name is Myles I like video games. I love the Holy Spirit.
I love to swim. I like the color blue and I like dogs,cats and baby pigs.

The questions I have for you are how hard is it to be a priest? How do you know that God wanted you to be priest?

Thank you for answering all my questions.

Sincerely,

Myles

ARCHDIOCESE
— OF —
SAINT PAUL &
MINNEAPOLIS

Dear Myles,

Thank you for your question. I love being a priest. I think that it would be hard to be a priest if we didn't have God's help — but with God's help, it's amazing what we are able to do. As the Angel Gabriel told Mary, "Nothing is impossible for God."

When God is calling a person to some particular service, He's going to give him or her the gifts that they will need. That's why it is so important that we ask God to help us know what He is calling us to do with our lives. When I was your age, I thought that God might be calling me to be a priest, but I didn't know until much later, when I was sent to a seminary in Rome. Even though I am not very good with languages, I saw that the Lord was blessing my efforts and helping me to learn, even though the classes were taught in Italian and Latin. I also saw that the Lord was increasingly placing in my heart a desire to be of service to others, even in situations that went outside my usual comfort zone. I took those as signs confirming my gut feeling that the Lord wanted me to be a priest.

+Bernard A. Hebda

Aimee-Rae

St. Michael Catholic School
Prior Lake, MN

Fourth Grade

"What was your childhood like?"

Dear Archbishop Hebda,

I heard you were looking for some questions you could answer. I was hoping you could answer some of mine. My name is Aimee-Rae Weaver. I go to Saint Michael Catholic School. My 4TH grade teacher is Mrs. Vochoska. I live in Lonsdale, MN. I am moving to Prior Lake (city) in April. I have two brothers and a sister. My family and I are very inspired by you. I was thinking you could help me understand my Catholic faith.

First of all, I'd like to ask you, what was your childhood like? I know there is a lot to tell when it comes to that, but I have been wondering for a while. I wonder if it is like mine. It would be nice to know.

Lastly, I'd like to thank you for your time, talent, and treasure. Thank you for letting me write a letter to you. I just want you to know that you have changed my point of view 100%! You are a true inspiration. So, thank you.

From your inspired Catholic,

Aimee-Rae Weaver

Dear Aimee-Rae,

I feel really blessed to have grown up in a great home with loving parents, a younger sister and two younger brothers. While I was a good bit older than my sister and brothers, they were always very good to me (and continue to be very kind to me).

We lived in a fun neighborhood in Pittsburgh with lots of kids. We would ice-skate and go sled riding in winter, play baseball in spring, swim and play tennis in summer, and play football in fall. We were blessed to have a great Catholic school in our neighborhood as well, with more than 1,600 students who all lived within walking distance of the school! I wish that every child could have a childhood like mine!

+Bernard A. Hebda

Mateo

Immaculate Conception
Catholic School
Columbia Heights, MN

Kindergarten

**"Do you behave yourself?
I have a hard time being
quiet in school."**

My name is Mateo Idrovo Cuesta. I am a Kindergartner at Immaculate Conception School in Columbia Heights. My sister Lucero goes to school here too. She is in fifth grade and her nickname is Lucky. I LOVE to play soccer and I am really good at it.

My question for you, Archbishop Hebda, is: Do you behave yourself? I have a hard time being super quiet in school. My favorite times in school are recess, gym and free choice time. I like to play!

Thanks for being our Archbishop. I hope I get to meet you someday soon.

Dear Mateo,

It sounds like we have a lot in common (even though I'm sure you're much better at soccer than I am). I never found it easy to be quiet in school and seemed to always get the giggles at the worst possible times.

I once was caught talking and had to write 100 times: "A wise old owl sat on an oak. The more he saw the less he spoke. The less he spoke the more he heard. We should be like that wise old bird." After that, I was much quieter!

+Bernard A. Hebda

Katie

Nativity of Our Lord
Catholic School
Saint Paul, MN

Second Grade

**"Is the bread and wine
really Christ's
Body and Blood?"**

Dear Bishop Hebda,

I am in second grade at Nativity of Our Lord School. I have an older brother and a younger sister. I am the middle child.

At school we are getting ready for First Communion. Is the bread and wine really Christ's body and blood?

Thank you,
Katie Nobrega

ARCHDIOCESE OF SAINT PAUL & MINNEAPOLIS

Dear Katie,

As Jesus Himself said of the bread that He offered at the Last Supper, "This is my Body," and of the wine, "This is my Blood." I cannot imagine a more reliable source. Every time that we go to Mass, we have the opportunity to receive the life-giving Body and Blood of Jesus. I hope that your first communion was a really special day for you.

Whenever we visit a Catholic Church, we actually have the opportunity to visit with Jesus, who waits for us in the Tabernacle. How special is that? It's probably easier to open our hearts to Jesus there than in any other place. We show that we believe that Jesus is truly present by being reverent when we come up for Holy Communion and by genuflecting whenever we pass by the Tabernacle.

+Bernard A. Hebda

Santiago

Nativity of Mary
Catholic School
Bloomington, MN

Second Grade

"Have you had other jobs than being an Archbishop? Do you like to cook? Do you like going on walks? What is your favorite show?"

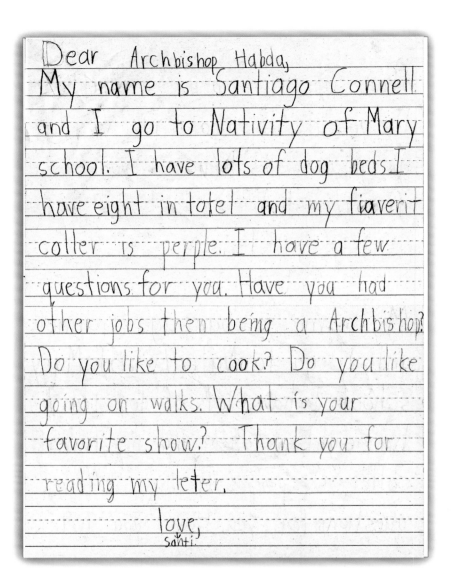

Dear Archbishop Habda,
My name is Santiago Connell and I go to Nativity of Mary school. I have lots of dog beds I have eight in totel and my fiaverit coller is perple. I have a few questions for you. Have you had other jobs then being a Archbishop? Do you like to cook? Do you like going on walks. What is your favorite show? Thank you for reading my leter.
love,
santi.

ARCHDIOCESE
OF
SAINT PAUL &
MINNEAPOLIS

Dear Santiago,

Before I was a priest, I worked as a lawyer, as a typist, as a dishwasher and in a children's library. I enjoyed all those jobs. I was never a cook, and that should make you happy. Even though I love to eat, I am a disaster in the kitchen.

In my spare time, I love to go on walks, whether in the city or in the country. I am a steady walker but not very fast.

As for my favorite TV show, I am a sucker for "The Voice." I often wonder what would happen if I had to get a chair to turn when I preached. Would I get to go on to the next round?

Ellen

St. Vincent de Paul
Catholic School
Brooklyn Park, MN

Second Grade

"What is something Jesus has blessed you with that you praise?"

Dear Archbishop Hebda,

Hello, I hope you are doing well. I wanted to introduce myself. My name is Ellen Cliff and I'm 8 years old. I go to St. Vincent de Paul Catholic church and I'm in 2nd grade. My teacher's name is Mrs. Folger. My favorite thing about school is read centers because I like to read Mrs. Piggle-wiggle. After school I like to read books and play with my dolls. I also have a question for you. What is something Jesus has blessed you with that you praise? I can't wait to hear from you!

Love,
Ellen Cliff

ARCHDIOCESE OF SAINT PAUL & MINNEAPOLIS

Dear Ellen,

I certainly praise God for blessing me with the opportunity to serve first as a priest, and then as a bishop, particularly in this Archdiocese. People often thank me for saying "yes" when I was asked to come to the Archdiocese, but I see it as a great blessing that speaks to me of God's great love. I know that I'm the one who should be grateful. If I hadn't come to Minnesota, I would have never met you and probably would have never heard about the Mrs. Piggle-Wiggle books. I would never be able to live in an upside-down house.

I was happy to hear that you like to read, and I hope that you will continue to enjoy books. My first job was at a children's library, and my boss used to get frustrated that I always wanted to read the books rather than put them away. I hope that you have found some good books about the saints.

+Bernard A. Hebda

God's Creation

Giovanni & Katherine

Risen Christ Catholic School
Minneapolis, MN

Second Grade

"Can you speak more about God and prayer and how do we love?"

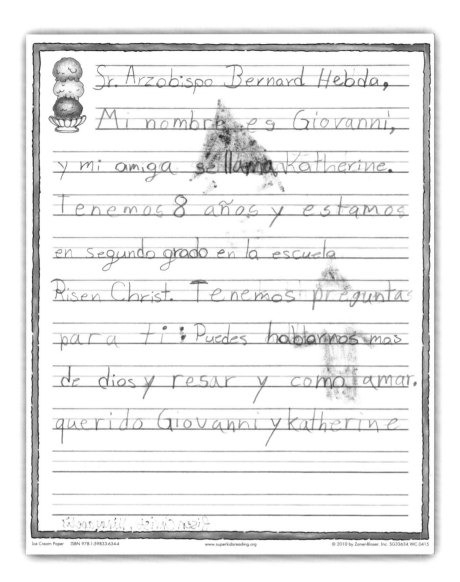

Sr. Arzobispo Bernard Hebda,
Mi nombre es Giovanni, y mi amiga se llama Katherine. Tenemos 8 años y estamos en segundo grado en la escuela Risen Christ. Tenemos preguntas para ti: Puedes hablarnos mas de dios y resar y como amar. querido Giovanni y katherine

100

ARCHDIOCESE
OF
SAINT PAUL &
MINNEAPOLIS

Dear Giovanni and Katherine,

I am jealous that you write so well in Spanish. I make way too many mistakes when I try to write in Spanish.

Thanks for your questions. I bet you already know that it is really important that we spend time talking with those we love, whether that be with our family or with our friends. That's how we keep our love strong and even grow in our love. That is true about our relationship with God as well. We need to talk with God every day (isn't that what prayer is?) if we want to keep our love strong.

The more we come to know about God from our prayer, the more that we know how He wants us to love others. By the way, I'm sure that God speaks Spanish.

+Bernard A. Hebda

Ashley

St. Vincent de Paul
Catholic School
Brooklyn Park, MN

First Grade

"How is Jesus a part of God?"

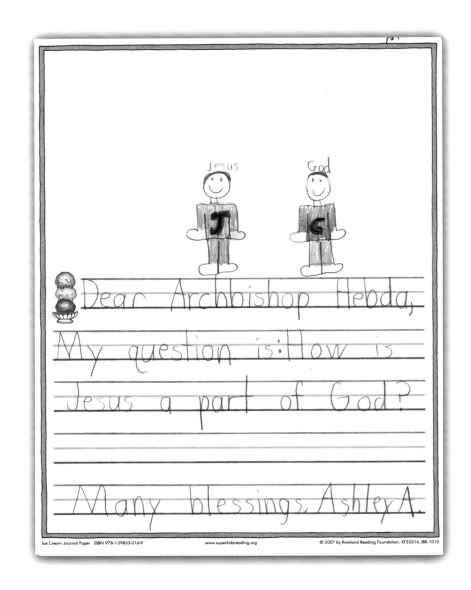

Dear Archbishop Hebda,

My question is: How is Jesus a part of God?

Many blessings, Ashley A.

God's Creation

Dear Ashley,

What a deep question for a first grader. Jesus is God's son. While He lived a life like yours and mine, and would have lost His baby teeth just like you, He was really and truly God. That became clear when He grew older. We read in the Bible that He did amazing things that only God can do, such as changing water into wine, walking on water and curing those who couldn't see or hear. We read that He rose from the dead and was able to love and forgive even those who hurt Him.

He spoke about God the Father in a very tender way and taught us to think of God as *our* father too. You can tell from the way that Jesus spoke about the Father and the Holy Spirit that He knows them really well and loves them very much. It's amazing that Jesus would want to share those relationships with us.

+Bernard A. Hebda

Melvin

St. Maximilian Kolbe
Catholic School
Delano, MN

First Grade

**"Why did God make
mosquitoes?"**

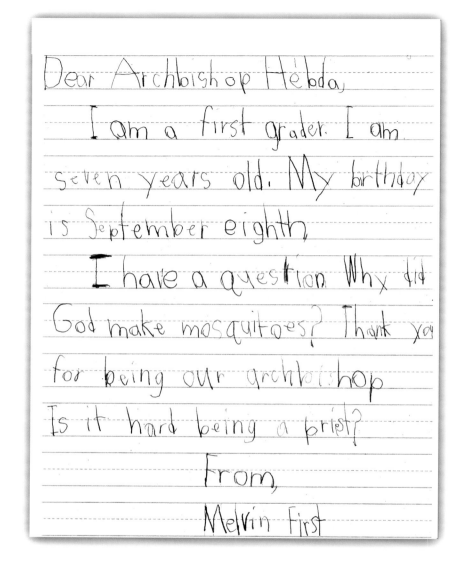

Dear Archbishop Hebda,

I am a first grader. I am seven years old. My birthday is September eighth.

I have a question. Why did God make mosquitoes? Thank you for being our archbishop.

Is it hard being a priest?

From,
Melvin First

Dear Melvin,

I loved your question and was really impressed that you could spell "mosquitoes" correctly. I always have to look it up in the dictionary.

I, for one, would not have complained if God had *not* made mosquitoes. I am pretty sure that He made them to remind me when I have overstayed my welcome at a cookout. I also think that God might have made mosquitoes to keep the bats happy. I read that the average bat can eat 1,200 mosquitoes an hour. Minnesota must be like heaven for a hungry bat.

+Bernd A. Hebda

Second Graders

Shakopee Area Catholic School
Shakopee, MN

Second Grade Students

"Do you ever get to celebrate Mass with school children? Does it get hard and lonely not having a family? What do you do with all of your free time?"

Dear Archbishop Hebda,

We are second grade students at Shakopee Area Catholic School. This year we are so excited to receive Jesus in the sacrament of First Eucharist in the spring. We received First Reconciliation during Advent.

We like gym, learning about multiplication and going to Mass on Wednesday. Do you ever get to celebrate Mass with school children? We learned that you are from Pittsburgh and we are wondering if you get to visit your family or if they come to visit you.

We also learned that you are ordained so you cannot be married. Does it get hard and lonely not having a family? What do you do with all of your free time?

Our class really enjoyed learning about you. There are lots of questions that we had so we are looking forward to reading your book to learn more about you.

Sincerely,

Mrs. Wermerskirchen's 2nd Grade

Dear Second Graders,

Thank you for your kind note. I love celebrating Mass for school children and hope that I will get invited to your school soon. I know that your school is one of the largest in our Archdiocese, so it would be fun for me.

I love visiting my family, especially since they live near a beach in Florida. We had a great time together this summer. They have already come to visit me in Minnesota, and I hope that they will come back many times. My nieces and nephews loved the rides at Mall of America.

I haven't been lonely one minute since I arrived in the Twin Cities. Our Archdiocese is very active, so there is always something to do, and I feel that God has really blessed me with the kindness of so many families here.

+Bernard A. Hebda

Jamison

St. Joseph Catholic School
Rosemount, MN

Fourth Grade

"Is it hard to give up everything for Christ and God? How do you do it? I pray four times a day. How many times do you pray in a day?"

Dear Archbishop Hebda,

My name is Jamison, and I love sports. I also like my school. I am in the best school ever. I love math. I am very good at it too. Soccer, baseball, and basketball are my favorite sports. I am very good at baseball, and I even got a traveling team. In basketball I am very good. We have some big games coming up, and I hope we do good. My parents are the best. They care for me, they give up everything for me and my sisters, and allow me to go to a Catholic school.

I have a question. Is it hard to give up everything for Christ and God? How do you do it? I pray 4 times a day. How many times do you pray in a day? What do you do when you are not praying and why? You do so much in my church, my school, the world, and my faith. How do you do so much? How did you get into such a good college? Is there a web site you recommend to Catholics so they can learn more about their faith?

God bless you,
Jamison Callahan

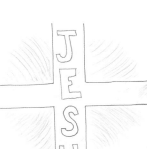

ARCHDIOCESE
OF
SAINT PAUL &
MINNEAPOLIS

Dear Jamison,

I'm impressed that you pray four times a day — that's great. What a wonderful way to stay close to Jesus. When we know how much He loves us, we know that He gives us way more than we give up for Him. That is certainly true in my life.

Like you, I enjoy praying. Priests get to pray by celebrating Mass every day, and then saying certain prayers in the morning, during the day, in the evening and then before we go to bed. Like you, we ask for God's blessing before we eat and thank God for providing us with what we need.

In our offices, we made sure that we have a chapel so I can pray before Jesus in the Tabernacle whenever I want. How cool is that?! While we know that God is everywhere and can hear us pray wherever we are, it has always been easiest for me to pray in a beautiful church or chapel before the Blessed Sacrament.

+Bernard A. Hebda

Gabrielle

Holy Spirit Catholic School
Saint Paul, MN

Kindergarten

"When people die do they turn into angels?"

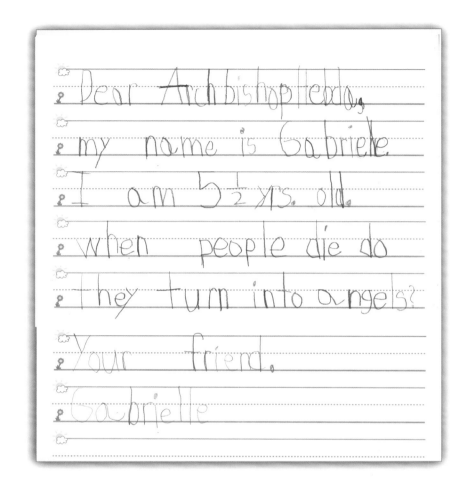

Dear Archbishop Hebda,
my name is Gabriele.
I am 5½ yrs. old.
when people die do
they turn into angels?
Your friend,
Gabrielle

ARCHDIOCESE
OF
SAINT PAUL &
MINNEAPOLIS

Dear Gabrielle,

I was really happy that you described yourself as my friend. I think friends are really important in life — and I am glad that you are one of them.

Just as dogs don't turn into cats, I don't think that people turn into angels. But once we die and are no longer weighed down by our bodies, I think that we will share many things in common with the angels.

I bet that you know you are named after one of the greatest of angels, the Archangel Gabriel. He is famous for being a messenger of God. It was Gabriel, for example, who told Mary that she would be the mother of God. The name "Gabriel" in Jesus' language means "God is my strength." I hope that you feel that God is your strength too.

+Bernard A. Hebda

Sion

St. Raphael Catholic School
Crystal, MN

First Grade

"Do you text?"

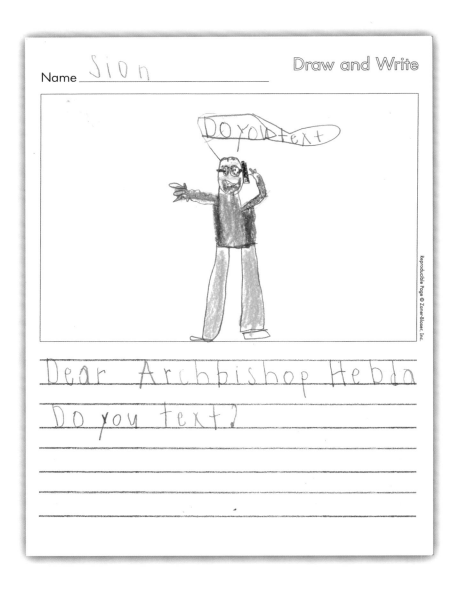

Name Sion

Draw and Write

Dear Archbishop Hebda
Do you text?

Dear Sion,

What a great name! Do you know that Sion was one of the names for Jerusalem, one of the cities where Jesus taught and where He died?

As for your question, I love to text, even though I'm not nearly as fast as my nieces and nephews. My thumbs don't move as quickly or as accurately as theirs. I'm also not so great at using emojis. Because I make so many mistakes, I was encouraged to use voice recognition to send texts, but I stopped after it called one of my priests "Father Rotten" instead of Father Rutten.

+Bernd A. Hebda

Adelaide

Way of the Shepherd
Catholic Montessori School
Blaine, MN

Kindergarten

"What is your favorite color?"

Deer Archbishup Hebda.
wut is yor fovrit culr?
I wil pray for you.

Love,
Adelaide Weisbecker
kindergardin

The Way of the Shepherd catholic Montessori

Dear Adelaide,

My very favorite color is green. I love that there are so many different shades of green and that priests often get to wear green at Mass.

I have to confess, however, that while green is my favorite color, I don't always like to eat things that are green. Lettuce, spinach, guacamole and mint chocolate chip ice cream are all great, but brussels sprouts and artichokes aren't my favorite. I wish that God had made them a different color.

+ Bernard A. Hebda

Vanel

St. Peter's Catholic School
Forest Lake, MN

First Grade

"Did Jesus dance?"

Dear Archbishop Hebda,

My name is Vanel. I am in First grade at St. Peter's School in Forest Lake. At school, I like to learn about rocks, reading, and science. I like to go sledding and to play. Other things I like to do are play school and play ball.

I have a question for you. I am wondering-did Jesus dance?

Thank you for reading my letter. I'm excited to be able to write to you. I hope you will answer my question. God bless you.

Vanel

ARCHDIOCESE
OF
SAINT PAUL &
MINNEAPOLIS

Dear Vanel,

You stumped me! I don't know for sure if Jesus danced, but I would guess that He did. Jesus lived a very ordinary life before He began His public ministry, and I bet He would have done the same kind of things that friends His age would have done.

We know from the Bible that Jesus was a guest at a wedding at Cana, and it would have been common for guests at a Jewish wedding to dance. I have a hard time picturing Jesus doing the Dougie or the Cupid Shuffle — but you never know.

+Bernard A. Hebda

Claire

Annunciation Catholic School
Minneapolis, MN

Kindergarten

"What is your favorite fruit?"

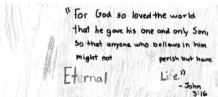  

ARCHDIOCESE
OF
SAINT PAUL &
MINNEAPOLIS

Dear Claire,

I have never met a fruit that I didn't like, and your drawings of an apple and a bowl of berries made me hungry. From the time I was your age, I have always gone crazy for strawberries. I like them plain, love them with whipped cream and am thrilled when I can enjoy them along with vanilla ice cream.

When I lived in Italy, we could also find mini-strawberries that were particularly great with lemon juice and sugar. No surprise — my favorite pie is strawberry-rhubarb pie.

My second favorite fruit would be figs, but they are not so common here in Minnesota.

+Bernard A. Hebda

Riley

Presentation of the Blessed
Virgin Mary Catholic School
Maplewood, MN

First Grade

**"How many hours a day do
you pray to Jesus?"**

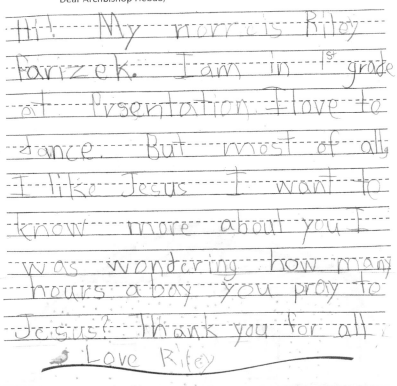

PRESENTATION
of MARY

Dear Archbishop Hebda,

Hi! My norre is Riley Farizek. I am in 1st grade at Presentation. I love to dance. But most of all, I like Jesus. I want to know more about you. I was wondering how many hours a day you pray to Jesus? Thank you for all.

Love Riley

ARCHDIOCESE
OF
**SAINT PAUL &
MINNEAPOLIS**

Dear Riley,

   I was thrilled to read that you love to dance but most of all, you like Jesus. When we love someone, we want to spend time with them, speak with them, get to know them, share our lives with them. When that person is Jesus, we do that in prayer.

   St. Paul tells us that we should "pray always." That doesn't mean that we can't do anything else, like play, study or work, but it means that we should make sure that we remember Jesus even when we are playing, studying or working. I try to do that by saying little prayers throughout the day. I put pictures of Jesus, Mary and the saints all around my office to remind me to do that, to remind me throughout the day that the work that I am doing is for Jesus and that I need to ask for His help. When people write to me about challenges in their lives, I try to remember to pray for them as I hold their letter. I'm not sure how many minutes or hours each day I spend in that kind of prayer.

   I know that in addition to those moments of prayer, I need to spend some time each day just with Jesus. I love to do that at Mass each day and then again united with the Church around the world for about 15 minutes each morning, evening, midday and night. I also try to pray quietly each day in the presence of Jesus, who waits for us in our churches and chapels. Because we give that time to the Lord, we call it a holy hour.

+Bernard A. Hebda

Bridget

St. Francis Xavier Catholic School
Buffalo, MN

Fifth Grade

**"Do you like being
Archbishop? Why?
If you had all the money in
the world, what would
you do?"**

Dear Archbishop Hebda,

Hello, my name is Bridget DesMarais, I am a fifth grader at St. Francis Xavier School. I love soccer, do piano, and love art! Right now we are learning about Mother Teresa, she is really cool. By the way you are my favorite Archbishop!

I love learning about you, and all the good you do. Do you like being Archbishop? Why? Also, If you had all the money in the world what would you do?

I hope you recieve my letter! I can't wait to hear your response!!!

God bless you...

Love,
Bridget

ARCHDIOCESE
OF
SAINT PAUL &
MINNEAPOLIS

Dear Bridget,

I really love being a priest — and being an Archbishop allows me to be a priest for lots of people so I am very happy. I never imagined that I would be a bishop or an Archbishop since they always seemed so old!

If I had all the money in the world, I would work to make sure that everyone had great doctors and enough to eat. I would also want to make sure that any child who wanted to go to a Catholic school like yours would be able to do so. It sounds like you are learning some amazing things in school. I am glad that you enjoyed learning about Mother Teresa, and you even spelled her name correctly.

+Bernard A. Hebda

Shayla

St. Mark's Catholic School
Saint Paul, MN

Fifth Grade

"Why did you go to law school? My mom is in law school."

Dear Archbishop Hebda,

    My name is Shayla Le, I am a student at Saint Mark's School. My brothers and I are on the swimming team, and go to karate, and choir for Saint Mark's. I also do dancing, gymnastics, and piano. I really like Saint Mark's because everyone's nice and the activities are so much fun!

    I'd like to know why you went to law school. My mom is going to law school because she wants to help others and she's always very busy. Every body has their reasons for things and I'd like to know yours. Also want to know if you enjoyed law school.

    Thank you because you did a lot of great things and it affected family in a way. Being in a Catholic schools the best, there's tons of fun and a lot of great people. Saint Mark's is the best, I'm happy to be a Catholic.

        From,
        Shayla Le

ARCHDIOCESE OF SAINT PAUL & MINNEAPOLIS

Dear Shayla,

I was delighted to hear that you are happy to be a Catholic. Me too! I'm glad that you are in the choir at St. Mark's School. When I visited your school, I was really impressed to hear you sing in Latin.

As for why I went to law school, my reason is the same as your mom's: I wanted to help people. Lawyers can really assist people who might not have a strong voice of their own. Lawyers work to make sure that people are treated fairly.

In order to make sure that lawyers are well prepared, law school can be pretty intense. Law students have to spend lots of time not only learning about our laws but also learning to think like lawyers. My years in law school were the busiest years of my life, but I really enjoyed them. I met some of my best friends there and learned with them how important it is to work hard. We also had a really good time together exploring New York City. Life there could be a little crazy. I lived above a fire department and across the street from a busy hospital — so I can sleep through anything.

+ Bernard A. Hebda

Grace

St. Jerome Catholic School
Maplewood, MN

Fifth Grade

"What is it like to be Archbishop? Why is there evil in the world? Why are people hungry?"

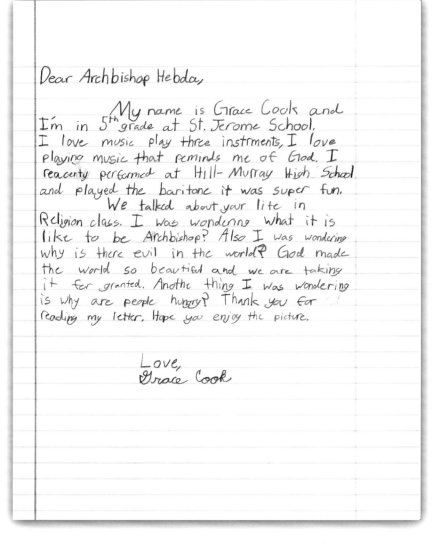

Dear Archbishop Hebda,

My name is Grace Cook and I'm in 5th grade at St. Jerome School. I love music play three instruments, I love playing music that reminds me of God. I reacenty performed at Hill- Murray High School and played the baritone it was super fun.

We talked about your life in Religion class. I was wondering what it is like to be Archbishop? Also I was wondering why is there evil in the world? God made the world so beautiful and we are taking it for granted. Anothe thing I was wondering is why are people hungry? Thank you for reading my letter, Hope you enjoy the picture.

Love,
Grace Cook

ARCHDIOCESE
OF
SAINT PAUL &
MINNEAPOLIS

Dear Grace,

      It sure sounds like God is doing great things in your life. It's hard to believe that you are already playing three musical instruments at your young age. How wonderful that you are using the gifts that God gave you.

      So far, being Archbishop has been very rewarding. To use your words, it has been "super fun." I feel honored to be serving in this Archdiocese.

      I also appreciated your questions about evil and hunger. I agree with you that God blessed us with a beautiful world that we sadly sometimes take for granted. Pope Francis has been reminding us that we really need to take care of our planet, to avoid unnecessary waste and to share the resources that we have. We are really blessed here in the United States and have to look for ways to help others. I'm always happy to hear about projects in our Catholic schools that help us to respond to the needs of others.

+Bernard A. Hebda

Charlotte

Holy Cross Catholic School
Webster, MN

Fourth Grade

"How many pilgrimages have you been on? How many schools have you said Mass at? How would you feel if you became the Pope?"

Dear Archbishop Hebda,

I am Charlotte Benolkin. I am a fourth grade student at Holy Cross Catholic School in Webster, Minnesota. I play mostly golf and tennis. My favorite subject in school is Math. I have two siblings that attend the same school as me and one sibling in high school, but she is on her way to college.

My first question is: How many pilgrimages have you been on? My second question is: How many schools have you said mass at? My third question is: How would you feel if you became the Pope?

Thank you so much for taking the time to read my letter. God bless you!

Sincerely,

Charlotte Benolkin

ARCHDIOCESE
OF
SAINT PAUL &
MINNEAPOLIS

Dear Charlotte,

I've been on more pilgrimages than I can count. I love visiting holy spots. My favorite pilgrimage was to Israel, the Holy Land where Jesus lived. Did you know that some people make pilgrimages to our cathedral, the National Shrine of the Apostle Paul?

Besides going to holy places, I love visiting Catholic schools. I think that I visited 32 of them last year, and I look forward to visiting more this year. I really enjoyed coming to your school for the dedication of your new chapel. Your school choir rocked!

As for how I would feel if I were named Pope — probably like you would feel if you were elected president of the United States. I think that I'm safe. It's been more than 600 years since someone not a cardinal has been elected Pope.

+Bernard A. Hebda

Elizabeth

Ave Marie Academy
Maple Grove, MN

Second Grade

"Why did Jesus send us to earth when he could send us to heaven instead?"

Dear Archbishop Hebda,
My name is Elizabeth and I am in 2nd grade at Ave Maria Academy in Maple Grove. My favorite class is History. I like to play soccer and read. Why did Jesus send us to earth when he could send us to heaven instead? Thank you for leading our church. God bless you!

Love Elizabeth

ARCHDIOCESE
OF
SAINT PAUL &
MINNEAPOLIS

Dear Elizabeth,

     What a great question! We need to remember that when God created Adam and Eve, earth was a paradise very much like what we imagine heaven to be. Everything was in harmony in the Garden of Eden. You might have noticed that there was no mention of homework in that part of the Bible. The garden was so perfect that God would come to walk there in the cool of the day! Imagine having the chance to bump into God and speak to Him face-to-face.

     By putting us on earth, God gives us the chance to work with Him to build something great out of His creation. I'm sure that heaven is perfect, but I'm really happy to have the chance to see the beauty of Minnehaha Falls.

+Bernard A. Hebda

Archbishop Bernard Hebda and teachers Steve Wright, Michelle Schlehuber and Jeanne Doyle pose with the Catholic school students whose letters are contained in this book.

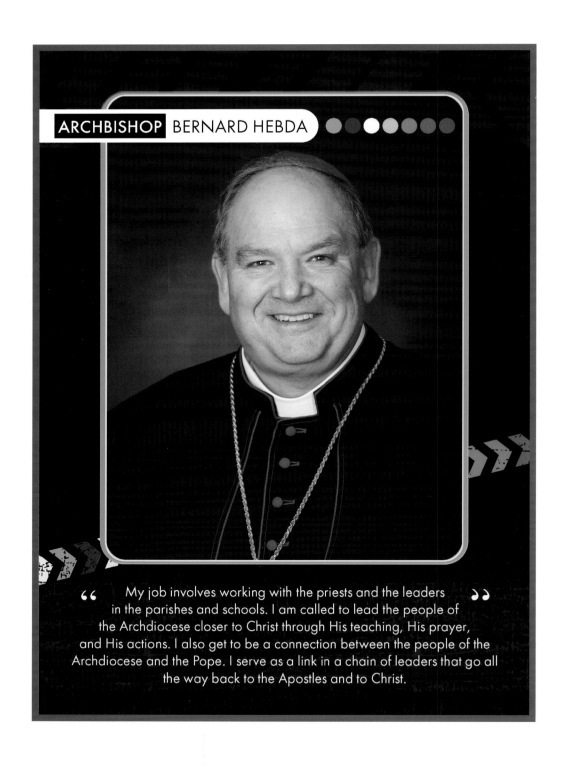

ARCHBISHOP BERNARD HEBDA

" My job involves working with the priests and the leaders
in the parishes and schools. I am called to lead the people of
the Archdiocese closer to Christ through His teaching, His prayer,
and His actions. I also get to be a connection between the people of the
Archdiocese and the Pope. I serve as a link in a chain of leaders that go all
the way back to the Apostles and to Christ. "

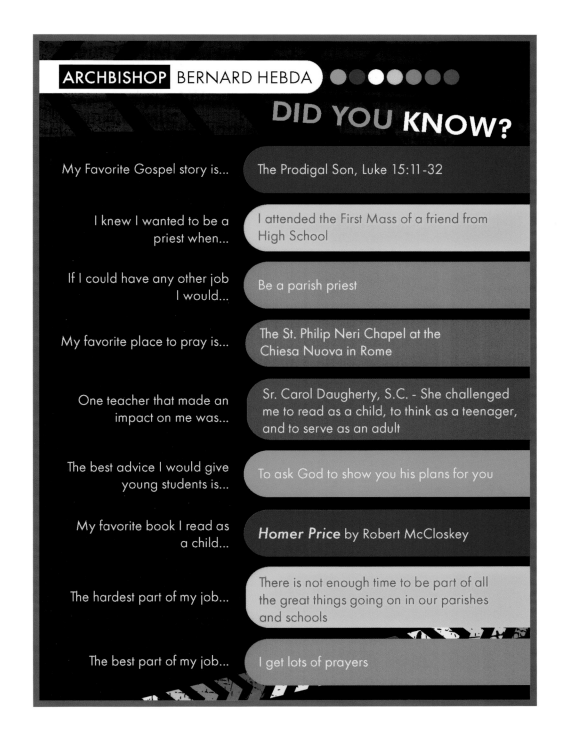

ARCHBISHOP BERNARD HEBDA

DID YOU KNOW?

My Favorite Gospel story is...
> The Prodigal Son, Luke 15:11-32

I knew I wanted to be a priest when...
> I attended the First Mass of a friend from High School

If I could have any other job I would...
> Be a parish priest

My favorite place to pray is...
> The St. Philip Neri Chapel at the Chiesa Nuova in Rome

One teacher that made an impact on me was...
> Sr. Carol Daugherty, S.C. - She challenged me to read as a child, to think as a teenager, and to serve as an adult

The best advice I would give young students is...
> To ask God to show you his plans for you

My favorite book I read as a child...
> *Homer Price* by Robert McCloskey

The hardest part of my job...
> There is not enough time to be part of all the great things going on in our parishes and schools

The best part of my job...
> I get lots of prayers

A Word From Our Friends

By: **LAURA SOBIECH**

My husband and I began the spiritual education of our children at home; when we were deciding where our children would be educated, we knew for certain we needed a school that would be our partner in building a solid foundation in truth. We found that partner in our local Catholic parish school.

With the constant clamor of enticing messages competing for our children's minds and hearts, being a Catholic parent in today's world was, and is, continuing to be a struggle.

The spiritual health of our children depends on the opportunities we provide to continually witness the faith lived out in the home and in their community. During some of our darkest days, when our son Zach was dying from bone cancer, our Catholic school community rallied around our family. They carried us through with countless deeds of practical support, like bringing us meals and sending gift cards. But they also carried us through with spiritual support by holding prayer vigils at our church adoration chapel and filling the church for Mass to pray for Zach and our family when things got really hard.

Not only do Catholic schools offer a superior education, but they infuse the understanding that the ultimate purpose for our intellect is to be in service of God and His will.

There, faith is an active part of daily school life, lived freely and without the constraints and distractions of the secular world. They lay the foundation for a lifelong journey toward a deeper, meaningful relationship with Jesus Christ and His Holy Church.

St. Croix Catholic School gave Zach the education that served as a stepping stone in his spiritual journey that ultimately helped him grapple with death. His teachers, friends and other faithful people served as witnesses of Christ's redemptive love that brought him and our family peace as he prepared his soul for heaven.

By: **MATT BIRK**

Asking questions is an essential part of learning. So often, when we try to teach young people, we think it's all about what we tell them or how we present information.

In reality, what's important is what they hear and how they receive the information. Being able to have questions answered is essential when trying to close this gap to ensure new ideas and concepts take root.

And that's where us adults come in. We need to stoke the fire of natural inquisitiveness that exists inside of our children. Their minds are free from conventional wisdom and skepticism, trying to figure out the world and, like the rest of us, on a quest for truth. Magic can happen when you feed this desire for knowledge with the breadth and depth of the Catholic faith.

A child's mind is fertile ground, and we need to make sure the seeds of the full truth can take hold. The more we understand our faith and our Church, the more we see its beauty.

Beauty speaks to the heart, and once it takes hold of the heart, you are Catholic for life.

I think this book is a great idea and a useful evangelization tool as we fight for the hearts and minds of our young people. I'm sure I will learn a lot by reading it. But don't tell my kids — I'm supposed to have all the answers.

Acknowledgments

Ask the Archbishop is based on the belief that religion is at its best when we are seeking answers to life's questions. While reading each of the hundreds of letters written to Archbishop Hebda by the children of our community, this belief was affirmed over and over again.

The journey to publication started with the seed of an idea, planted in the summer of 2016, that has been nurtured and cultivated by many people. We owe so much to Gail Dorn, Maureen Lodoen and Melissa Hamilton of Catholic Schools Center of Excellence for their unflagging enthusiasm and support for this project. We are so grateful for them! Thank you, also, to Jim Bindas for his editing talent and expertise, and to Danielle Rother for her graphic design artistry.

We are so grateful to our Visitation School community, for their unwavering support and encouragement, from start to finish. Our administration and teaching teams gave us the time, space and resources we needed to develop this idea into the book it has become. Their Salesian Spirit and generosity are incomparable.

We so appreciate all of the principals and teachers in the Archdiocese of Saint Paul and Minneapolis who embraced this project, took time to offer this opportunity to their students, and sent back a selection of letters and artwork. We truly wish we could have included all of the beautiful artwork and heartfelt letters!

We owe a tremendous thank you to the Most Reverend Bernard Hebda, our beloved Archbishop. Without his generous involvement, we would not have this beautiful book. From our very first meeting, he approached this project with an open heart. He answered our every request with a "yes." Each answer he has given in the pages of this book is honest, thoughtful, inspiring and touching. His wisdom, grace and leadership are deeply appreciated.

Last, but by no means least, we thank the children whose hearts are revealed to us here.

To bring some of the youngest members of our faith community together with our Archbishop in conversation and celebration is a dream come true for us.

– Michelle Schlehuber, Steve Wright and Jeanne Doyle

Tillie P.